Crystal
Pendulum for
Dowsing
An ancient knowledge for
unlocking Psychic Power

Robert W. Wood
(Diploma in Hypnotherapy)

Rosewood Publishing

First published in U.K. 2002
By Rosewood Publishing
P.O. Box 219, Huddersfield,
West Yorkshire HD2 2YT

www.rosewood-gifts.co.uk

Revised cover and
Re-printed in 2004
Again in 2011

Robert W Wood D.Hp
Asserts the moral right to be identified
As the author of this work

Copy-editing
Margaret Wakefield BA (Hons) London
www.euroreportage.co.uk

Cover photograph by
Andrew Caveney BA (Hons)
www.andrewcaveneyphotography.co.uk

Cover and layout re-designed by
AJ Typesetting
www.ajtype.co.uk

Printed in Great Britain by
Delta Design & Print Ltd
www.deltaleeds.co.uk

ISBN 978-0-9532930-4-9   BK5

CRYSTAL PENDULUM FOR DOWSING

The purposes of a man's heart are
deep waters,
but a man of understanding
draws them out.

Proverbs 20 : 5

Discovering a Miracle for Self-Help

Dowsing

Crystal pendulum dowsing is born from an art which in itself dates back many thousands of years. Mention dowsing to most people, and images of traditional diviners seem to come to mind - of men and women walking along through fields of green, holding with both hands a forked twig, one that looks a little like a wish-bone and seems to always be pointing upwards.

It's affectionately called a 'twitch', probably because it starts to 'twitch' just before it changes direction when it gets near to water, oil, minerals, gold or whatever the diviner may be looking for at the time.

Although hazel is probably the most popular material used, it seems to work just as well with ash, green elder or willow; even whalebone and common plastic have been used quite effectively.

Dowsing can also be done with other tools. A good example is a pair of metal rods bent into an `L' shape. It doesn't seem to matter what kind of metal the rods are; the dowser holds one in each hand, just as he would if they were a pair of guns, and when water - or any other substance he is dowsing for - is located, the rods move and cross over. This then marks the spot.

How does dowsing work?

There seem to be three schools of thought. One is that the dowser creates a bridge between the logical and the intuitive part of the mind, that is: the conscious (logical), and the subconscious (intuitive).

Another, that the dowser connects with a higher power, that is: that the information is coming from a 'divine' source, hence the name 'divining'.

Others say that it is electromagnetic energy, radiating from everything, that causes the effect. However, personally I fail to understand how a wooden or a plastic object can be influenced by an electromagnetic energy.

No one may know for certain, but I am going with the idea that there's a link with the conscious and subconscious mind. I think we will be on much safer ground.

Dowsing - a natural gift

In my opinion, the ability to dowse is a simple, natural gift of the human spirit, present in each one of us from birth. It's a simple method of bringing our rational consciousness safely into direct communication with our inner wisdom, our intuition, our subconscious. Although this may be difficult to understand at first, it will become clearer when you discover that the subconscious part of the mind is in some respects the most truly primary sense of all. It's certainly, you're about to discover, the most powerful.

Dowsing, then, is, when focused, a discipline that can help bridge the gap between the two levels of mind, the conscious and the subconscious, our inner and outer world. Our consciousness could be easily compared to the visible part of an iceberg, which everybody knows is only a tiny part of the whole. In fact, nine-tenths of an iceberg is below the surface.

Dowsing potentially gives us a means to have unlimited access to information, information which would normally be invisible and well out of view to the human eye, certainly well beyond the limitations of our five senses. Once you can dowse, you will find it possible to detect all sorts of things. It's like the difference between having a computer, and a computer that's connected to the internet.

Crystal Pendulums

New tools have been introduced over the years for dowsing, and especially, more recently, the crystal pendulum*. For the purpose of simple diagnosis for health, or gaining extra help for wealth, love, energy etc, the crystal pendulum is by far the most practical. It has the advantages of being very portable and easy to handle (much better than having to carry a large, forked stick in your pocket).

* A full range of crystal pendulums are available on-line at www.rosewood-gifts.co.uk

A priest's discovery

Whilst I was researching into dowsing, I came across this story, of a priest who, on his return from Ireland, had become very excited about his discovery of divining rods. Apparently whenever he prayed, the rods seemed to twist in his hands and cross over. He found this so exciting that he showed his parishioners, and in fact anybody else he thought might be interested. One of his parishioners, not feeling too comfortable about this, wrote to the Church and asked whether the Church encouraged or permitted this.

Now when push comes to shove, the shortest answer would probably be 'no', and indeed the answer did come back as 'no'. The reason given was that dowsing is a form of divination (the art or practice of discovering future events or unknown things as though by supernatural powers) and divination, as far as this Church was concerned, was occult and therefore must be forbidden.

So any practice that resembles it must be dealt with using extreme caution. The answer went on to explain that a prayer before or while using the divining rods might, in itself, render the practice innocuous; but it was still not recommended.

If one is trying to get supernatural information, then it is definitely, according to this explanation from the Church, of the occult. However, I don't think that's how the priest had seen it, nor do many others. You must judge for yourselves, but you are about to discover just how natural all this really is.

To help you experience what you are about to discover, I would like you to experience for yourselves this natural phenomenon. To help, read the following instructions and then try them out before you read any more. This will help you towards your discovery of a 'knowing'.

A Pendulum

In my book *Discover Why Crystal Healing Works*, I use pictures. One such picture shows a young woman who can also look very old, a little like a witch. Another shows a staircase that moves as you look at it. The front cover of my book shows an obelisk; when you look straight at it you can see only hieroglyphics written along it, but if you tilt your head you can see a word. These effects can be quite disturbing if you are not aware of what is happening. But remember: in all cases, the effect is being shown to you to help you understand the power you hold within your mind. This technique is a very powerful, effective way of exciting the imagination, which in my opinion holds the key. I will now show you how to use a pendulum to produce the same effect as the pictures.

The following instructions are taken from my book *Create a Wish Kit Using a Candle, a Crystal and the Imagination of Your Mind* ('Wish Kit' for short).

Get a weight and tie it onto the end of a piece of string, so that you can use it like a pendulum. I have found that a simple key, like a Yale key, works just as well. You may have a crystal pendulum; this is even better. Now get a piece of paper, say A4 size, and draw a circle on it using a small saucer. Next, around the circumference put four dots, as if you were marking out a clock at twelve, three, six and nine o'clock. Then connect the dots, making a cross; the point where the lines cross is the centre of the circle, and it's going to be a target. Place the paper on a table, sit down, and make yourself comfortable.

Hold the pendulum over the centre of the target. Steady it, if you have to, by allowing the pendulum to touch base, then lifting it just a little so that it is able to swing freely under the influence only of gravity. If you are uncomfortable, place your elbows onto the table to help support your arms. Whatever you do, DO NOT MOVE. Now, using only the power of your mind, imagine the pendulum swinging back to front, or swinging in a circular motion, either clockwise or anticlockwise. If it's not going in the direction you want, then imagine it changing direction; and it will. It may be slow at the beginning. But it will change, and you will get better at it with practice. Try it - I know you'll be astounded. Remember, I am only showing you this effect to help you understand the principles behind this power within the mind.

A 'knowing'

Can you ride a bike? I know it may seem a daft question, and I bet you're wondering what it's got to do with crystal pendulums, but for a moment humour me. So, can you ride a bike? I'll assume the answer to be 'yes'. Then - what was the difference from the moment you couldn't to the moment you could? It's a rhetorical question, because I think the answer is 'knowing'. Somehow, you seem to know you can.

It's like learning to drive a car: a little experience, some instruction, some effort, and hey-presto! you've passed the test. A few weeks later you're driving like everybody else. Something's kicked in, and I think it's a good example of this 'knowing'. Another example of this 'knowing' is: When you can drive a car, you consciously decide where you're going to go - 'I am going from here to there' - but you can't drive a car consciously. You need to drive it using your subconscious. You drive automatically - and you only have to see a learner driver learning to drive to understand what I mean. You can see them having to consciously 'think' about mirrors, brakes, clutch, gears, steering, signals, etc, etc. There's just too much information to be taken in consciously; however, when the subconscious takes over with this 'knowing', it takes everything in its stride and driving becomes very comfortable. It's strange, I don't think there will ever be a computer that can drive a car like a human being can. Therefore this 'knowing' is more powerful than any computer that has ever been built, or is likely to be. Other examples of 'knowing' could be swimming, typing, etc.

It's easier to learn how to drive a car than it is to learn how to build one. But just imagine if you did know how to build one; it would come in very useful if you ever broke down. My intention is, with this book, to give you a useful anchor, so if you ever do 'break down', you'll have the tools at hand to do a self-repair. I am going to guide you to a 'knowing'.

I've often heard it said that we shouldn't dabble in things we don't understand. However, by learning, and gaining knowledge, we can open the prison doors of ignorance and fear and enter into a life described by St Paul as 'the glorious liberty of the sons of God'. This freedom is gained when we have discovered our 'knowing'.

Beware of misconceptions

I recall an occasion when I was giving a talk to a ladies' luncheon group. My talk was entitled 'Discover the hidden powers of gemstones'*, and it had been well publicised. One of the ladies came up to me just before I was due to speak and told me she would have liked to have stayed and listened to me. However, she had apparently mentioned to one or two people at her church, in all innocence, how she was looking forward to hearing a speaker talk on what she thought would be a fascinating subject, but then was surprised to find that they seemed to object, and even went a stage further and suggested she didn't come.

On hearing this I explained that it was OK by me, and that my advice to her was that if it would make her feel uncomfortable in any way, then she should leave. Then she noticed I was wearing a Christian fish on my jacket. Although a little confused, she decided to stay, and so with some of her non-church friends she stayed and listened to me.

After my talk, she came over and told me how much she had really enjoyed it, especially the way I had linked Christianity and 'new age'. She then went on to say that she had made a decision regarding her own church. "I've decided," she said, "I am not going to tell them that I stayed." The fact that I had been talking in a kind of coded language about God's power didn't seem to have helped. It was apparently my use of the word 'hidden' that they had objected to.

What's in a word?

I discovered, years ago, that just one word on my posters was causing me no end of trouble, and once I changed it, the problem just vanished. The original line on my poster was: 'LEARN ABOUT BIRTHSTONES AND THE ORIGINS OF ASTROLOGY AS WE NOW KNOW IT'. Although it took me nearly two years to discover it, it was the word 'Astrology' that some, mainly within the church, objected to, so I changed the word and the line to: DISCOVER A CONNECTION BETWEEN BIRTHSTONES AND THE SCRIPTURES' and I haven't had any problems since.

* Now available on CD. Contact publisher or go online to www.rosewood-gifts.co.uk for further details.

Occult or Psychic?

Although the word 'occult' means 'hidden', not everything that's hidden is necessarily occult.

> **There is nothing concealed that will not be disclosed,**
> **Or hidden that will not be made known.**
>
> Luke 12:2

Psychic ... outside the possibilities defined by natural laws, as mental telepathy, sensitive to forces not recognised by natural laws, esoteric. Mental as opposed to physical.

Psychic speaks of apparent non-physical, yet human powers that emerge under certain circumstances and conditions. These could be primarily telepathy, clairvoyance and precognition (the ability to foresee future events). I believe we can include healing powers, and the faculties of dowsing as well. Another instance is the ability to see auras of colour or light around the human body.

Occult ... of or characteristic of mystical or supernatural phenomena or influences. Beyond ordinary human understanding, secret or hidden.

The word 'occult', on the other hand, suggests contact with spirit powers, black magic and witchcraft - all of which the author would seriously warn against. Most people will have heard of the 'Ouija Board'. It's a trademark for a board on which are marked the letters of the alphabet. Answers to questions are spelt out by a pointer and are supposedly formed by spirits. It isn't a coincidence that sometimes one of the questions asked at a preliminary interview before commencing psychotherapy is, whether the client has ever played with a Ouija board. I would place the Ouija board firmly into the occult category.

Natural psychic power

After reading the above descriptions, I hope you will agree with me that 'pendulum dowsing' falls safely into the realms of psychic power. I believe it to be natural and one of the most accurate ways of connecting back to the inner self, whilst being at the same time the safest - safe because there's no third party involved to misinterpret. We are using our own inner 'wisdom'. There is no break in the connection between the inner and outer worlds of the mind.

When asked about electricity, Thomas Edison is said to have replied: "I don't know what it is, but it's there, so let's use it."

Let's start by discovering our psychic power so we can help ourselves with our personal development, our dreams, our goals. Never forget that there is a power within, and that it can be summoned at any time and in any situation.

Just as radios receive information via unseen airwaves, so our minds act in the same way: our powerful antenna receives information from the vibrations and energy waves being continuously emitted by people, places, thoughts and things.

Throughout all the ages, man has striven in various ways to express his inner needs. The more simple and sincere he is in his wishes, hopes and prayers, the more successful he seems to be.

You can't get a much greater simplicity than the ability to dowse; it's a special natural gift of creation. For many, dowsing is a recognised method of bringing together the conscious mind (the 'gate keeper') and the subconscious (the 'inner child').

Some have described tapping into this 'inner world', the world of the subconscious, as like tapping into a rich vain of pure gold. Dowsing seems to be a way of bridging the conscious and subconscious parts of our minds whilst at the same time being able to sidestep the intellect.

Crystal dowsing therefore becomes an external expression of the internal. It's the visible bringing together of the mind and the spirit. Although dowsing may be thought of as an art or even a science, dowsing is really more 'holistic'; that is, a connection between the mind, body and spirit.

Illustration by Rachel Lubinski

10

Removing the intellect

The intellect is that part of the mind housed within the consciousness. It's the part of the mind that says, "This is all nonsense, this can't be, these things just don't happen." It's the adult speaking. It needs to respond intellectually, to always to give an explanation as to why.

This is one reason why the psychotherapist uses hypnosis to shut down this faculty. For psychotherapy to work, it's best if the intellect isn't there. Let me give you an example. A client says that they have an irrational fear or phobia of closed-in spaces, and they need help because they have just landed a position with a new company. Their office is on the fifteenth floor and because they're scared of closed-in spaces, they can't use the lift. They know they're being silly but they do need help. Then the intellect steps into the conversation and goes on and explain it's probably because their brother locked them in the broom cupboard when they were three.

However, let me say here and now that if a client ever says they know why they have irrational fears and phobias, but they are still having them, then the reason they give is not the original cause of their problems. There is a 'law of cause and effect' (trust me, I am a hypnotherapist!).

"I tell you the truth, anyone who will not receive the Kingdom of God like a little child will never enter it."
Luke 18 -17

Was psychotherapy around all those years ago? I wonder.

Having been asked when the Kingdom of God would come, Jesus replied, "The Kingdom of God does not come visibly, nor will people say 'Here it is' or 'There it is', because the Kingdom of God is within you." Luke 17 : 20-21.

Our subconscious mind can be likened to that of a child.

The basic principles

At its simplest, crystal dowsing involves asking questions to help seek out information not readily available by any other means.

You are about to discover that the uses for dowsing are only limited by our imagination.

When we ask our 'dowsing question', we are asking with our intellectual, rationally-thinking, conscious part of the mind. We ask a clear, unambiguous question in our mind. Then, having asked, we wait for the reply - a little like waiting for an internet search.

The answer, when it comes, comes in the form of movement. The crystal pendulum will begin to move either from side to side or from back to front, or even circling clockwise or anti-clockwise.

This is the external expression of our inner world - the inner world of the subconscious - where you'll find intuition, our sixth sense. From the previous experiment you will be quite familiar with the pendulum movements. Now we will learn how to interpret these movements, and it couldn't be easier.

It's not a panacea

Do you suffer from medical problems that won't respond to medical treatment? Do you feel that your luck's just run out? Can't find the right partner, however hard you look? Need to gain more energy, change your career, your life-style? Although you may not believe this, your problems could be being caused by repressed emotions, by incorrect subconscious thinking. The following may help to show if the true cause of your problems resides within your mind. Although crystal dowsing is not a panacea, you're about to discover how it can go a long way towards helping.

**Start here by tuning into your psychic energy
for your personal development and well-being.**

Instructions

Although it's not strictly necessary to sit or stand in a special way, a good posture often helps to relax.

Hold the cord of your pendulum between the thumb and forefinger, just as if you were holding a plate, in your dominant hand. (That is your right hand if you are right-handed, or left if left-handed). In my crystal healing demonstrations I always suggest that for best results the healing crystals should be held in the passive hand, so as to receive.

You will by now, after following the 'Wish Kit' instructions, realise that pendulums respond and move in regular patterns, either from left to right, or front to back, either circularly clockwise or anti-clockwise.

We are now ready to start our communications by asking some simple questions so as to learn the meaning of the responses. We need to ask questions for which there's a clear, unambiguous 'yes' or 'no' response.

When the pendulum becomes still and stops swinging, then ask a question to which you know the answer can only be 'yes'. Ask the question out loud or as a thought within your mind, both methods are equally effective.

Make the questions simple, for example: 'My name is ...,' and say your name; or 'Today's day is ...,' and name the day; or 'My shoes are ... ' and name the colour; you get the idea! Make a note of the direction, ask a few more 'yes' questions and confirm the pendulum still travels in the same direction. This then becomes your 'yes' response. Repeat it all again for a 'no' response. If you find you are getting inconsistent responses - stop, relax and start again.

Try some exercises

From this point you can play some games to exercise your new-found knowledge. Ideally, practice exercises in dowsing should be fun and engaging; after all, you are communicating with your inner wisdom, the subconscious, the part some call the 'inner child'.

For these exercises you're asking questions to which the answers can only be 'yes' or 'no'. Any ambiguity will only make the exercise very difficult to follow.

For example, start with a simple hiding game such as hiding a ball under a cup and dowsing to find its position. Playing cards can be a very good exercise. Take an ordinary pack of cards, take out the jokers, shuffle the pack and then lay them out face down. Using the pendulum, start by identifying whether the top card belongs to the black or red suits. Place your pendulum over the card and ask clearly in your mind, "Does this card belong to one of the black suits?" It's either a 'yes' or a 'no' response. Go through the whole pack, then see just how close you came. Remember, we are trying to establish a connection with a part of ourselves that will have been dormant for quite a long time, so we can afford to be patient and take the time to wake it up slowly and gently.

Once we are clear about our responses and familiar with the use of the pendulum, we can start to use dowsing on a regular basis in our everyday life.

Become your own psychic investigator

Whatever your problems seem to be, why not start by checking if you are the victim of unconscious, self-limiting, negative conditioning? Now you are becoming familiar with crystal dowsing as a technique for communicating with the subconscious, start by asking questions. For example: "Is my (name the problem or symptoms) due to an event from my past that still troubles me or upsets me in any way?" "Is my (name the problem or symptoms) due to an event from my past that has conditioned me to respond in this way?" I would ask the question a few times to check the response, and change the way the question is formulated. **Remember: you should always consult your medical practitioner or advisor. Crystal dowsing should not become the only method of diagnosing your problems.**

To help you, here's a little more information as we delve deeper into the mind. The more you know, the greater your freedom. Here's more of a 'knowing'.

Brain waves

For all the advances of modern society, we cannot afford to ignore the ancient rhythms of the brain within all of us, any more than we could neglect our need to eat or sleep. Our state of mind is important for our dowsing to be effective, and the most powerful states of mind for our purposes here are Alpha and Theta.

Alpha and Theta are terms used in psychology to represent the various states of the mind when recording the brain waves. Alpha and Theta are probably the best states for relaxation, hypnotherapy, subliminal persuasion, and auto-suggestion. It's the state of mind just before we go to sleep or just after we have woken up. We can add to this our experience of pendulum dowsing.

There are four main frequencies that have been categorised: Beta, Alpha, Theta and Delta. Beta brain waves are associated with normal physical and mental activities whilst awake. Alpha waves are associated with deep relaxation, ideal for crystal dowsing. Theta waves are associated with dreaming, meditation and the experience of entering or coming out of sleep. The slowest and deepest, Delta waves, are associated with dreamless sleep, a somnambulist state.

Nature and sleep

It's said that only the fittest will survive, and because there's ruthless competition for limited resources, our planet could easily be described as a dangerous place to be. Yet the most spectacularly successful species of them all, human beings, spend almost a third of their lives paralysed and senseless - and no, I am not talking about after a good night out; I am talking about sleep.

Strange how the most advanced animals, normally watchful, shrewd and alert, drop their defences to sleep. It must mean that there's a huge benefit for all of us in sleep, or surely the powerful forces behind nature would have eliminated sleep a long time ago. Although it may have been risky sometimes to sleep, it must mean sleep is very valuable. So take a leaf out of nature's book: be as relaxed as possible when using your crystal pendulum for dowsing.

Gaining knowledge from hypnosis
In the phenomenon of hypnotism, as it is understood psychologically, there are numerous situations in which our senses are deceived by what the mind is directed to see, feel or hear during an extreme state of suggestibility.

Follow my thinking here, because I believe that, by looking at the crystal dowsing phenomena from a different angle - science and psychology - you will gain a further `knowing'.

We have often witnessed stage hypnotists demonstrating, for example, that if they suggest to a subject that an ordinary coin being held in the hand is getting red-hot, immediately the coin will be dropped, because the person involved will say he felt his fingers being burned. Such examples of 'mind over matter', as they are called, are really commonplace in psychology.

Hypnotism was used in the beginning in surgery. It was suggested to the person that he was insensitive to pain. Hypnotism was employed very successfully for surgical anaesthesia before the discovery of ether. Can you see just how powerful the forces are that are at work here? Turn it on its head, and you'll see the kind of power that's working through the pendulum.

Chevreul's Pendulum
Michel Eugene Chevreul (1786 -1889) was a French chemist, a director at the Natural History Museum in Paris, and a man noted for his extensive researches.

He investigated mediums and clairvoyants, and the apparently inexplicable movements of the pendulums that they used to use. By a series of experiments, Chevreul proved that although people could have been acting in all good faith, the movements of the pendulum were actually caused by almost imperceptible muscular movements of the hand holding the thread; in other words, although the subjects were completely unaware of the unconscious movements of their hands, the pendulum's movements were caused by involuntary movements on the part of the individual holding the pendulum.

You can now turn this fact to your advantage, because it means the movements must be coming from the subconscious - your inner wisdom - and not the intellect, the conscious.

Mystery and Imagination

I have used this 'knowing' effect quite spectacularly at my party plan demonstrations when we are having 'an evening of mystery and imagination'. To make a point, I use the description in my book 'Wish Kit' to demonstrate this 'knowing' by using a pendulum. I tell my volunteer to hold a pendulum in their hands, and, whatever they do, not to move, but, using only the power of their mind, to imagine the pendulum moving in any direction they want. And when it does, they think it's spooky.

Is it spooky?

You should by now realise it isn't spooky, but quite natural, although at parties you can cut the atmosphere with a knife! In fact, the volunteer will often drop the pendulum and even move away from it.

It's all in the state of mind.

"Your intelligence is always with you, overseeing your body, even though you may not be aware of its works.
Rumi (1207 -1273)

A journey to wholeness

As we begin to trust and integrate our new-found knowledge - a gift from the spirit within - we will gradually find that if we are growing, we need to use tools, such as crystal pendulums for dowsing, less and less. We start to become increasingly secure in a profound sense of our inner 'knowing' of a sense of rightness, of well-being, of tuning into an inner peace. We find ourselves naturally and intuitively choosing to do what our bodies, minds and spirits need to do, for stimulation and to guide us to inner contentment. We then find ourselves celebrating in self-expression and fulfilment, in the sure knowledge of our spirit's existence and its purpose.

**"Live the journey,
the journey is Life"**

Other titles in the 'POWER FOR LIFE' series:

Discover your own Special Birthstone and the renowned Healing Powers of Crystals REF. (BK1) A look at Birthstones, personality traits and characteristics associated with each Sign of the Zodiac – plus a guide to the author's own unique range of Power Gems.

A Special Glossary of Healing Stones plus Birthstones REF. (BK2) An introduction to Crystal Healing, with an invaluable Glossary listing common ailments and suggesting combinations of Gemstones/Crystals.

Create a Wish Kit using a Candle, a Crystal and the Imagination of Your Mind REF. (BK3) 'The key to happiness is having dreams; the key to success is making dreams come true.' This book will help you achieve.

Gemstone & Crystal Elixirs – Potions for Love, Health, Wealth, Energy and Success REF. (BK4) An ancient form of 'magic', invoking super-natural powers. You won't believe the power you can get from a drink!

Crystal Healing – Fact or Fiction? Real or Imaginary? REF. (BK6) Find the answer in this book. Discover a hidden code used by Jesus Christ for healing, and read about the science of light and colour. It's really amazing.

How to Activate the Hidden Power in Gemstones and Crystals REF. (BK7) The key is to energise the thought using a crystal. The conscious can direct – but discover the real power. It's all in this book.

Astrology: The Secret Code REF. (BK8) In church it's called 'Myers Briggs typology'. In this book it's called 'psychological profiling'. If you read your horoscope, you need to read this to find your true birthstone.

Talismans, Charms and Amulets REF. (BK9) Making possible the powerful transformations which we would not normally feel empowered to do without a little extra help. Learn how to make a lucky talisman.

A Guide to the Mysteries surrounding Gemstones & Crystals REF. (BK10) Crystal healing, birthstones, crystal gazing, lucky talismans, elixirs, crystal dowsing, astrology, rune stones, amulets and rituals.

A Simple Guide to Gemstone & Crystal Power – a mystical A-Z of stones REF. (BK11) From Agate to Zircon, all you ever needed or wanted to know about the mystical powers of gemstones and crystals.

Change Your Life by Using the Most Powerful Crystal on Earth REF. (BK12) The most powerful crystal on earth can be yours. A book so disarmingly simple to understand, yet with a tremendous depth of knowledge.

All the above books are available from your local stockist,
or, if not, from the publisher.

NOTES

Welcome to the world of Rosewood

An extract from a 'thank- you' letter for one of my books.

"I realised just how much you really had indeed understood me and my need for direction and truly have allowed me the confidence and strength to know and believe I can achieve whatever I want in life"

If you like natural products, hand-crafted gifts including Gemstone jewellery, objects of natural beauty – the finest examples from Mother Nature, tinged with an air of Mystery – then we will not disappoint you. For those who can enjoy that feeling of connection with the esoteric nature of Gemstones and Crystals, then our 'Power for Life – Power Bracelets could be ideal for you. Each bracelet comes with its own guide explaining a way of thinking that's so powerful it will change your life and the information comes straight from the Bible. e.g. read Mark 11: 22

We regularly give inspirational talks on Crystal Power – fact or fiction? A captivating story about the world's fascination with natural gemstones and crystals and how the Placebo effect explains the healing power of gemstones and crystals – it's intriguing. And it's available on a CD

To see our full range of books, jewellery and gifts including CD's and DVD'S

Visit our web site - www.rosewood-gifts.co.uk

To see our latest videos go to 'You Tube' and type in Rosewood Gifts.